Life crushes the soul and art reminds you that you have one

Life crushes the soul and art reminds you that you have one

Life crushes the soul and art reminds you that you have one

Life crushes the soul and art reminds you that you have one

Life crushes the soul and art reminds you that you have one

Life crushes the soul and art reminds you that you have one

Life crushes the soul and art reminds you that you have one

Life crushes the soul and art reminds you that you have one

Life crushes the soul and art reminds you that you have one

Life crushes the soul and art reminds you that you have one

Life crushes the soul and art reminds you that you have one

Life crushes the soul and art reminds you that you have one

Life crushes the soul and art reminds you that you have one

Life crushes the soul and art reminds you that you have one

Life crushes the soul and art reminds you that you have one

Life crushes the soul and art reminds you that you have one

Life crushes the soul and art reminds you that you have one

Life crushes the soul and art reminds you that you have one

Life crushes the soul and art reminds you that you have one

Life crushes the soul and art reminds you that you have one

Life crushes the soul and art reminds you that you have one

Life crushes the soul and art reminds you that you have one

Life crushes the soul and art reminds you that you have one

Life crushes the soul and art reminds you that you have one

Life crushes the soul and art reminds you that you have one

Life crushes the soul and art reminds you that you have one

Life crushes the soul and art reminds you that you have one

Life crushes the soul and art reminds you that you have one

Life crushes the soul and art reminds you that you have one

Life crushes the soul and art reminds you that you have one

Life crushes the soul and art reminds you that you have one

Life crushes the soul and art reminds you that you have one

Life crushes the soul and art reminds you that you have one

Life crushes the soul and art reminds you that you have one

Life crushes the soul and art reminds you that you have one

Life crushes the soul and art reminds you that you have one

Life crushes the soul and art reminds you that you have one

Life crushes the soul and art reminds you that you have one

Life crushes the soul and art reminds you that you have one

Life crushes the soul and art reminds you that you have one

Life crushes the soul and art reminds you that you have one

Life crushes the soul and art reminds you that you have one

Life crushes the soul and art reminds you that you have one

Life crushes the soul and art reminds you that you have one

Life crushes the soul and art reminds you that you have one

Life crushes the soul and art reminds you that you have one

Life crushes the soul and art reminds you that you have one

Life crushes the soul and art reminds you that you have one

Life crushes the soul and art reminds you that you have one

Life crushes the soul and art reminds you that you have one

Life crushes the soul and art reminds you that you have one

Life crushes the soul and art reminds you that you have one

Life crushes the soul and art reminds you that you have one

Life crushes the soul and art reminds you that you have one

Life crushes the soul and art reminds you that you have one

Life crushes the soul and art reminds you that you have one

Life crushes the soul and art reminds you that you have one

Life crushes the soul and art reminds you that you have one

Life crushes the soul and art reminds you that you have one

Life crushes the soul and art reminds you that you have one

Life crushes the soul and art reminds you that you have one

Life crushes the soul and art reminds you that you have one

Life crushes the soul and art reminds you that you have one

Life crushes the soul and art reminds you that you have one

Life crushes the soul and art reminds you that you have one

Life crushes the soul and art reminds you that you have one

Life crushes the soul and art reminds you that you have one

Life crushes the soul and art reminds you that you have one

Life crushes the soul and art reminds you that you have one

Life crushes the soul and art reminds you that you have one

Life crushes the soul and art reminds you that you have one

Life crushes the soul and art reminds you that you have one

Life crushes the soul and art reminds you that you have one

Life crushes the soul and art reminds you that you have one

Life crushes the soul and art reminds you that you have one

Life crushes the soul and art reminds you that you have one

Life crushes the soul and art reminds you that you have one

Life crushes the soul and art reminds you that you have one

Life crushes the soul and art reminds you that you have one

Life crushes the soul and art reminds you that you have one

Life crushes the soul and art reminds you that you have one

Life crushes the soul and art reminds you that you have one

Life crushes the soul and art reminds you that you have one

Life crushes the soul and art reminds you that you have one

.

Life crushes the soul and art reminds you that you have one

Life crushes the soul and art reminds you that you have one

Life crushes the soul and art reminds you that you have one

Life crushes the soul and art reminds you that you have one

Life crushes the soul and art reminds you that you have one

Life crushes the soul and art reminds you that you have one

Life crushes the soul and art reminds you that you have one

Life crushes the soul and art reminds you that you have one

Life crushes the soul and art reminds you that you have one

Life crushes the soul and art reminds you that you have one

Life crushes the soul and art reminds you that you have one

Life crushes the soul and art reminds you that you have one

Life crushes the soul and art reminds you that you have one

Life crushes the soul and art reminds you that you have one

Life crushes the soul and art reminds you that you have one

Life crushes the soul and art reminds you that you have one

Life crushes the soul and art reminds you that you have one

Life crushes the soul and art reminds you that you have one

Life crushes the soul and art reminds you that you have one

Life crushes the soul and art reminds you that you have one

Life crushes the soul and art reminds you that you have one

Life crushes the soul and art reminds you that you have one

Life crushes the soul and art reminds you that you have one

Life crushes the soul and art reminds you that you have one

Life crushes the soul and art reminds you that you have one

Life crushes the soul and art reminds you that you have one

Life crushes the soul and art reminds you that you have one

Life crushes the soul and art reminds you that you have one

Life crushes the soul and art reminds you that you have one

Life crushes the soul and art reminds you that you have one

Life crushes the soul and art reminds you that you have one

Life crushes the soul and art reminds you that you have one

Life crushes the soul and art reminds you that you have one

Life crushes the soul and art reminds you that you have one

Life crushes the soul and art reminds you that you have one

Life crushes the soul and art reminds you that you have one